Symbols of America

Titus Schorr

Rosen REAL READERS

Rosen Classroom™
New York

My name is James.
I am learning about American symbols in school.

This is the American flag.
It has 50 stars and 13 stripes.
The stars are for the 50 states.
The stripes are for the first
13 colonies.

This is the Great Seal of the United States. There is an eagle on the seal. The eagle holds an olive branch in one foot. It holds arrows in the other foot.

The bald eagle is our national bird.

The bald eagle is not really bald. It has white feathers on its head.

America's motto is,
"In God We Trust."
You can find the motto on
paper money.
It is also on coins.

The President lives in the White House. The President works in the White House, too. The White House is in Washington D.C.

The Liberty Bell is in Philadelphia.
It was used to call people
to meetings.
There are four cracks in the bell.

The Statue of Liberty is in New York.

It was given to America as a gift from France.

Mount Rushmore is in South Dakota. It is a large sculpture of four presidents. Their faces are carved into a mountain.

I like learning about
American symbols.
There are many more to
learn about!
Let's learn some more!

Words to Know

bald eagle

flag

Great Seal

Liberty Bell

Mount Rushmore

Statue of Liberty